— PRAISE FOR —

The First Vision

"While some critics may question why there are differences among existing accounts of Joseph Smith's First Vision, these variations actually help us have a more complete understanding and appreciation of this transcendent event. Matthew B. Christensen, who has served as a bishop and a member of a stake presidency, has spent years studying the writings of Joseph Smith in depth. The harmony in this book, which blends ten known accounts of the First Vision, will make a meaningful contribution to your appreciation of the latter-day Restoration."

—*Dr. Richard O. Cowan*, Professor of Church History and Doctrine, Brigham Young University

"Rats! This is a book I always wanted to write. Fortunately, my jealousy has been replaced with elation and appreciation for a job well done. In much the same way I have always valued being able to read the four Gospels in harmony and do the same with the three accounts of the Apostle Paul's conversion, I had always felt that blending the contemporary accounts of the Palmyra theophany would prove to be both fascinating and spiritually enriching. And so it has. Matthew Christensen has rendered a major service to Latter-day Saints, as well as to persons of other faiths who realize how significant the First Vision is to their Mormon associates. This short work will be read and reread many, many times. It's a keeper and I recommend it highly."

—*Robert L. Millet*, Professor Emeritus of Religious Education, Brigham Young University

"The varying accounts of the First Vision have puzzled many readers in recent years. What really happened? Matthew Christensen has blended ten accounts of the First Vision, following the pattern of the useful harmonization of the four Gospels. The aim in both cases is to integrate apparently conflicting stories. The result here not only reconciles differences but greatly enriches our understanding of the First Vision."

—*Richard L. Bushman*, author of *Joseph Smith: Rough Stone Rolling*

THE FIRST

VISION

THE FIRST

VISION

A HARMONIZATION OF 10
ACCOUNTS FROM THE SACRED GROVE

MATTH TENSEN

The cover art of this book was created by Walter Rane and is entitled "The Desires of My Heart."

This is not an official publication of The Church of Jesus Christ of Latter-day Saints. The opinions and views expressed herein belong solely to the author and do not necessarily represent the opinions or views of Cedar Fort, Inc. Permission for the use of sources, graphics, and photos is also solely the responsibility of the author.

ISBN 13: 978-1-4621-1504-4

Published by CFI, an imprint of Cedar Fort, Inc.
2373 W. 700 S., Springville, UT 84663
Distributed by Cedar Fort, Inc., www.cedarfort.com

LIBRARY OF CONGRESS CATALOGING-IN-PUBLICATION DATA

Christensen, Matthew B., 1976- author.
The First Vision / Matthew B. Christensen.
pages cm
Includes bibliographical references.
ISBN 978-1-4621-1504-4 (alk. paper)
1. Smith, Joseph, Jr., 1805-1844--First Vision. 2. Church of Jesus Christ of Latter-day Saints--History--19th century. 3. Mormon Church--History--19th century. 4. Church of Jesus Christ of Latter-day Saints--Doctrines. 5. Mormon Church--Doctrines. I. Title.

BX8695.S6C55 2014
289.3092--DC23

2014020152

Cover and page design by Shawnda T. Craig

Edited by Kevin Haws

Printed in China

10 9 8 7 6 5 4 3 2 1

Printed on acid-free paper

— DEDICATION —

For Bryan T. Christensen and Joseph Fielding McConkie, two courageous men who loved Joseph Smith and his successors and taught me by word and deed what it means to be true to the message of the Father and the Son in the Sacred Grove.

CONTENTS

— ACKNOWLEDGMENTS —

Though a legion of family members, friends, and mentors have all contributed in different ways to the creation of this book, I alone am responsible for its contents.

Special appreciation is extended to Alexander L. Baugh, Richard E. Bennett, Randall J. Christiansen, Richard O. Cowan, Robert Freeman, Alonzo L. Gaskill, Steven C. Harper, W. Jeffrey Marsh, Joseph Fielding McConkie, Robert L. Millet, Mark D. Palmer, Kelly Reeves, and John W. Welch. My friend RoseAnn Benson is to be especially thanked for over a decade of encouragement in making this book a reality. Lyle Mortimer and the Cedar Fort staff have been incredibly professional and kind, and my gratitude is particularly directed to Catherine Christensen, Shawnda Craig, Rebecca Greenwood, Kevin Haws, and Kelly Martinez.

I am deeply grateful to my parents, Bryan and Carol Christensen, for their example of faith and testimony from my earliest years. Most of all, I express my most profound love and appreciation to my beautiful wife and muse, Talia S. Christensen, and our four precious children: Grace, Clark, Ella, and Gwyneth. They each helped me in the preparation of the manuscript and are my constant examples of Christlike living.

INTRODUCTION

"Joseph, this is My Beloved Son. Hear Him!"

With these words, our Heavenly Father announced the unsealing of the heavens, the opening of the dispensation of the fulness of times, and the calling of a prophet to once again reveal His Son to His children on earth. These words are readily familiar to those who believe in the divine commission of Joseph Smith. During his ministry, the Prophet Joseph publicly and privately shared his experience in the grove of trees we now call Sacred. Joseph referred to his theophany as the "first visitation."[1] To those who revere the Prophet, that singular moment in the early spring of 1820 is known as the First Vision.

There are ten known accounts of the First Vision that were written or published during the lifetime of the Prophet.[2] Initially, Joseph was hesitant to share his experience in the Sacred Grove.

However, as time went on and he gained spiritual experience, he began to share. As Richard L. Bushman observed, "As Joseph became more confident, more details came out."[3] This book seeks to harmonize elements of those accounts into a single narrative. Readers will be introduced to the various accounts in a unique and interesting way, and for some this will be their first encounter with the various accounts. Each account provides unique details, and seeing them as one reveals the First Vision in a new light. This harmony of the First Vision is intended to teach, testify, rekindle faith in the inaugural event of the Restoration, and stimulate interest in learning more about the different accounts. In addition, this harmony will demonstrate the unity that exists among the various accounts.

— CRITERIA —

When a person learns there are multiple accounts of the First Vision, there are typically two types of reactions. One reaction is to become cynical and wonder why he or she has never been made aware of them before. Furthermore, when this person learns there are differences among the accounts, a crisis of faith may develop. The other typical reaction is to become excited and devour the different accounts and see them as additional proof for the truthfulness of the restored gospel. It is hoped that this book will be a positive experience for all who read it.

This harmony only includes the First Vision accounts written during the lifetime of Joseph Smith—those written or recorded before June 27, 1844. There are a few reasons for this. Joseph could have had access to most of these accounts and could have corrected them had there been egregious mistakes. The secondary accounts would have been written down with the experience fresh in the mind of the recorder. There are additional accounts available for study and reflection that were written by others after the Prophet's martyrdom.[4]

Each of the ten accounts is important in its own way. Five of the ten are considered primary sources because they were either personally written or dictated by the Prophet himself. The remaining five are secondary accounts written by the Prophet's contemporaries after having heard him share the experience he had in the Sacred Grove. It is possible—and hoped—that one day additional contemporary accounts of the First Vision will be discovered and will shed further light on the inaugural visitation of this dispensation.

— THE ACCOUNTS —

Below are brief backgrounds of the ten accounts that are in this harmonization.[5] Each summary begins with the year the account was written and its author or originator.

1832, Joseph Smith.[6] This is the first known attempt of Joseph Smith to record[7] his experience as well as the "rise of the church of Christ in the eve of time."[8] The majority of this history was written in the summer of 1832[9] by the Prophet's scribe Frederick G. Williams, though only the portion that included the account of the First Vision is in Joseph Smith's personal handwriting.[10]

1835, Joseph Smith.[11] A man known as Robert Mathias or Matthews, a Jewish minister,[12] visited with the Prophet Joseph on the morning of 9 November 1835.[13] During the visit, the Prophet shared his First Vision, and this account is a record of what he said. It was recorded by Warren Parrish, a scribe for the Prophet, and it was later re-recorded into the Prophet's journal by another scribe, Warren A. Cowdery.[14]

1838, Joseph Smith.[15] The most familiar and only canonized account of the First Vision is found in Joseph Smith—History in the Pearl of Great Price.[16] Several different people were involved in the recording of this account. It was originally written by George Robinson, a scribe, and Sidney Rigdon, under Joseph Smith's direction. It was later copied by James Mulholland and then edited by Howard Coray, again under the supervision of Joseph.[17] Though this account would eventually become part of the first edition of the *History of the Church*, it was first published in the *Times and Seasons* in 1842, and then in the Pearl of Great Price by Franklin D. Richards in 1851 for the Saints living and serving in England.[18] Explaining why this particular account has been so familiar to Church members for so long, noted historian and pioneer of First Vision studies James Allen wrote, "It is evident that the Prophet intended this narrative to become the basic source for Church literature. . . . With such a purpose in mind, to set the record straight once and for all, it is likely that Joseph would more carefully consider this account than he had the earlier versions."[19]

1840, Orson Pratt.[20] Orson Pratt's 1840 pamphlet, *A Interesting Account of Several Remarkable Visions and of the Late Discovery of Ancient American Records,* contained the first published account of the First Vision.[21] Of additional interest is the intent of the publication: missionary work and spreading the message of the Restoration.[22] Pratt, a member of the Council of Twelve Apostles since its organization on 14 February 1835[23] and a trusted friend of the Prophet Joseph Smith, doubtless had occasion to personally hear the Prophet share details about the First Vision. Pratt's pamphlet, published while serving a mission in Edinburgh, Scotland, would later be published in books in the United States and sold as a pamphlet in Nauvoo.[24] Though Pratt's version includes details not found in primary accounts, "some of his additions find corroboration in other accounts."[25] Because Brother Pratt's telling of the experience is so similar to Joseph Smith's 1832 account, it is likely Brother Pratt had access to that account as he prepared his pamphlet for publication.[26]

1841, Joseph Smith.[27] This First Vision account was discovered in 2005 and is largely unknown.[28] The scribe, Howard Coray, was employed from 1840–41 by Joseph Smith as his clerk to help compile letters and history.[29] It is evident that Coray copied this account from a previous draft history, due to the nearly identical word structures and phrasing. Though Coray's account offers few "substantive"[30] differences from the official 1838 history that would eventually be canonized, the differences that do exist contribute enough interesting changes not found in other accounts that they are included in this harmonization. Based on a statement signed by Coray and accompanying the papers from which this account is taken, these changes are presumed to have been made by Joseph himself. Coray's statement reads, "These hundred pages of History were written by me, under Joseph the Prophet's dictation."[31]

1842, Orson Hyde.[32] Orson Hyde, also an original apostle and confidant of the Prophet, published a pamphlet to be used in European missionary work. This version of the First Vision found in Hyde's pamphlet is notable because it is the first time the account appeared in print in a foreign language. It was published under the title, *Ein Ruf aus der Wüste, eine Stimme aus dem Schoose der Erde* (*A Cry from the Wilderness, a Voice from the Dust of the Earth*). Like with Orson Pratt, we can safely assume that Hyde heard the First Vision experience directly from Joseph.

A comparison of Hyde's publication with Pratt's reveals enough similarities to suggest Hyde may have relied heavily on Pratt's 1840 publication as a source, but Hyde's pamphlet has enough differences to qualify as a separate account of the First Vision and is therefore used in this harmony.

1842/1843, Joseph Smith.[33] This account is a key element in a well-known LDS document known as the "Wentworth Letter," written by the Prophet in 1842. Though the information relating to the First Vision is modest, this account contains unique aspects not found in other accounts. The letter was written to John Wentworth,[34] editor of the *Chicago Democrat*. A friend of Wentworth, John Barstow, who was writing a history of New Hampshire, inquired about the Mormon Church, and Wentworth wrote the Prophet asking for information.[35] The text of the Wentworth Letter was published by I. Daniel Rupp in 1843 when Rupp wrote Joseph Smith, asking for an account of Mormonism to be included in a book he was preparing about religions.[36] Though this account appeared in two separate contemporary publications in the Prophet's lifetime, because the texts are identical, they are considered to be one account in this harmony.

1843, Levi Richards.[37] Levi Richards was an active member of the Church, and this account is found in his diary under the date of 11 June 1843.[38] Though little is known about the entry other than what was recorded, it was presumably written shortly after Richards heard the Prophet share his experience.

1843, David White.[39] This account was in a newspaper article by David Nye White, senior editor of the *Pittsburgh Weekly Gazette*, and was based on his interview with the Prophet in August 1843. The article first appeared in the 15 September 1843 issue of the *Gazette*[40] and was reprinted the following week in the *New York Spectator*.[41]

1844, Alexander Neibaur.[42] This account is from the journal of a Church member in Nauvoo, Alexander Neibaur. According to the entry, Neibaur recorded this the same day he heard the Prophet teach it at his home on 24 May 1844.[43] Neibaur was a German convert, immigrant, and a trained dentist,[44] and he tutored Joseph Smith in both Hebrew and German in Nauvoo.[45]

METHOD AND ORGANIZATION

To help identify which account of the First Vision is being quoted in the harmony, each account has been assigned a unique color. Every page of the harmonization has a key to correlate the account with its color. The official canonized version of the First Vision found in the Pearl of Great Price is in standard black ink, making it readily identifiable to the reader. Because this account is familiar, it will serve as the core melody in this harmony while the rest of the accounts will serve as accompaniment. In order to prevent unnecessary duplication when language from a lesser-known account is similar to that used in the 1838 account, preference is given to the lesser-known account, and the deleted word from the 1838 account is noted in the endnotes. The remaining nine accounts are in various colors that should be unique enough not to be confused with other accounts in the harmonization. As mentioned earlier, only the 1832 account was personally written by the Prophet Joseph, and readers may be interested to note when this particular account is being utilized by its color.

To improve the readability of the harmony, much of the grammar, spelling, and punctuation has been standardized. This amalgamation is neither to compare original documents nor to manufacture a First Vision account that pretends to be historical. Though it is hoped that people from all walks of life and backgrounds will find the harmony interesting and useful, the current academic standard of preserving the original documents as they were recorded with misspellings and grammatical errors has not been followed. As needed, pronouns in the Orson Pratt and Orson Hyde accounts have been changed from the third person to the first person, so as to have the Prophet telling the story. Gray-colored brackets and text identify any added or modified words or punctuation in order to help the flow of the experience. These editorial decisions are intended to help the reader and should not change the original intent of the author of the account. Out of necessity, the various accounts have been edited and removed from their original order and context to harmonize with the 1838 Joseph Smith—History account.

— LIMITATIONS —

The reader will note that the synthesis of ten different versions of the same history is a difficult task. When a conductor stands to lead the instruments in an orchestra, the main task is to create a setting in which all the various instruments can play together to achieve a symphonic harmony. Conducting a symphony is no simple undertaking. Likewise, arranging the various accounts of the First Vision has taken time, effort, and thought. Underscoring everything was a deep desire to be true to each account and treat the First Vision with the sacred reverence it warrants. Judgment calls have been made and certain elements were selected for inclusion over others. To paraphrase the ancient Book of Mormon prophet Moroni, if there are faults, they are mine (Mormon 8:17). Shortly after he wrote his 1832 account of the First Vision, Joseph Smith wrote W. W. Phelps and referred to his inadequate writing ability. He described his lack of skills as a "little narrow prison—almost as it were total darkness of paper, pen, and ink—and a crooked, broken, scattered, and imperfect language."[46] The author can sympathize.

In a letter to Elder Wilford Woodruff, Elder George A. Smith wrote the following of his amalgamations of the Prophet Joseph Smith's various discourses for publication in the *History of the Church*: "The greatest care was taken to convey the ideas of the Prophet's style as near as possible; and in no case was the sentiment . . . varied that I know of."[47] That same care has been taken

in harmonizing these ten contemporary accounts. Though this harmony is not perfect, perhaps it will provide the reader with a desire to become better acquainted with the original documents and see the First Vision from a new but faithful vantage point.

The harmonization, one hopes, walks softly through the Sacred Grove and the foundational moment of the Mormon experience. There are natural limitations to an endeavor such as this. The harmonization is not a replacement or a substitute for the historically documented accounts of the First Vision—nor does it presume to be. No records exist of the Prophet Joseph Smith having ever shared his experience in the Sacred Grove in the manner that this harmonization presents. Instead, this is a conflation of accounts that are considered historically accurate.

When dealing with primary and secondary accounts of a historical event like the First Vision, it is well to understand that not all sources are created equal. Though this harmony makes use of all ten contemporary First Vision accounts, some used herein are naturally more reliable than others. Because the five firsthand recitals were written or dictated by Joseph Smith himself, they are considered the most reliable versions. The general consensus is that the remaining five secondary accounts were recorded by people who did their best to be true to what they heard the Prophet say. It should be noted, however, that a historian who did much to lay the groundwork of seriously studying the various accounts and introducing them to a Churchwide membership wrote, "People who heard [the First Vision from Joseph Smith] were obviously impressed with different details and perhaps even embellished it a little with their own literary devices as they retold or recorded it."[48] With that in mind, it is hoped that the harmonization will serve as an additional witness to Joseph's experience with each element adding interesting and enlightening details to our personal and collective understanding of the First Vision.

— KEY —

To aid the reader in visually identifying whose account is being read at any moment, the following key has been prepared. As mentioned earlier, the gray text in brackets is added to assist the readability of the harmony in some places. The key will also appear at the bottom of each page to aid the reader.

Blue = 1832, Joseph Smith

Green = 1835, Joseph Smith

Black = 1838, Joseph Smith

Brown = 1840, Orson Pratt

Orange = 1841, Joseph Smith

Teal = 1842, Orson Hyde

Red = 1842/1843, Joseph Smith

Purple = 1843, Levi Richards

Aqua = 1843, David White

Lavender = 1844, Alexander Neibaur

Gray = added for ease of reading

THE DESIRES OF MY HEART ***by Walter Rane***

THE FIRST VISION

JS—H 5 Some time in the second year after our removal to Manchester,[1] there was in the place where we lived an unusual excitement on the subject of religion. It commenced with the Methodists, but soon became general among all the sects in that region of country. Indeed, the whole district of country seemed affected by it, and great multitudes united themselves to the different religious parties, which created no small stir and division amongst the people, some crying, "Lo, here!" and others, "Lo, there!" Some were contending for the Methodist faith, some for the Presbyterian, and some for the Baptist.

JS—H 6 For, notwithstanding the great love which the converts to these different faiths expressed at the time of their conversion, and the great zeal manifested by the respective clergy, who were active in getting up and promoting this extraordinary scene of religious feeling, in order to have everybody converted, as they were pleased to call it, let them join what sect they pleased; yet when the converts began to file off, some to one party and some to another, it was seen that the seemingly good feelings of both the priests and the converts were more pretended than real; for a scene of great confusion and bad feeling ensued—priest at war with and contending against priest, and convert against convert; so convincing an unprejudiced mind[2] that all their good feelings one for another, if they ever had any, were entirely lost in a strife of words and a contest about opinions.

JS—H 7 I was at this time in my fifteenth[3] year. My father's family was proselyted to the Presbyterian faith, and four of them joined that church, namely, my mother, Lucy; my brothers Hyrum and Samuel Harrison; and my sister Sophronia.

JS—H 8 During this time of great excitement my mind was called up to serious reflection and great uneasiness[;] I made the subject of religion an object of much study and reflection. [I] became seriously impressed with regard to the all important concerns for the welfare of my immortal soul. I began to reflect upon the importance of being prepared for a future state of existence: but how, or in what way, to prepare [my]self, was a question, as yet, undetermined in [my] own mind. [I] perceived that it was a question of infinite importance and that the salvation of [my] soul depended upon a correct understanding of the

Blue = 1832, Joseph Smith | Green = 1835, Joseph Smith | Black = 1838, Joseph Smith
Brown = 1840, Orson Pratt | Orange = 1841, Joseph Smith | Teal = 1842, Orson Hyde

same; [I] saw, that if [I] understood not the way, it would be impossible to walk in it, except by chance; and the thought of resting [my] hopes of eternal life upon chance, or uncertainties, was more than [I] could endure. But though my feelings were deep and often poignant, still I kept myself aloof from all these parties, though I attended their several meetings as often as occasion would permit. In process of time my mind became somewhat partial to the Methodist sect, and I felt some desire to be united with them; but so great were the confusion and strife among the different denominations, that it was impossible for a person young as I was, and so unacquainted with men and things, to come to any certain conclusion who was right and who was wrong. It also occurred to [my] mind that God was the author of but one doctrine, and therefore could not acknowledge but one denomination as his church; and that such denomination must be a people who believe and teach that one doctrine (whatever it may be) and build upon the same. [I] then reflected upon the immense number of doctrines now in the world, which had given rise to many hundreds of different denominations.

JS—H 9 My mind at times was greatly excited, the cry and tumult were so great and incessant. [I] wanted to get religion too[; I] wanted to feel and shout like the rest but could feel nothing. The Presbyterians were most decided against the Baptists and Methodists, and used all the powers of both reason and sophistry to prove their errors, or, at least, to make the people think they were in error. On the other hand, the Baptists and Methodists in their turn were equally zealous in endeavoring to establish their own tenets and disprove all others.

JS—H 10 In the midst of this war of words and tumult of opinions, I often said to myself: What is to be done? Who of all these parties[,] whose feelings toward each other all too often were poisoned by hate, contention, resentment and anger[,] are right; or, are they all wrong together? If any one of them be right, which is it, and how shall I know it? After [I] had sufficiently convinced [my]self to [my] own satisfaction that darkness covered the earth and gross darkness [covered] the people, [I] abandoned the hope of ever finding a sect or denomination that was in possession of the pure truth. The great question to be decided in [my] mind, was—if any one of these denominations be the Church of Christ, which one is it? Until [I] could become satisfied in relation to this question, [I] could not rest contented. I pondered many things in my heart concerning the situation of the world of mankind: the contentions and divisions, the wickedness and abominations, and the darkness which pervaded the minds of mankind. My mind became exceedingly distressed[,] for I [had] become convicted of my sins. The only alternative that seemed to be left was to read the scriptures and endeavor to follow their directions. [I] accordingly commenced perusing the sacred pages of the Bible with sincerity, believing the things that [I] read. By searching the scriptures I found that mankind did not come unto the Lord but that they had apostatized from the true and living faith and [that] there was no society or denomination that built upon the Gospel of Jesus Christ as recorded in the New Testament. And I felt to mourn for my own sins and for the sins of the world, for I learned in the scriptures that God was the same yesterday, today[,] and forever, that He was no respecter to persons, for He was God. For I looked upon the sun—the glorious luminary of the earth—and also the moon rolling in their majesty through the heavens, and also the stars shining in their courses, and the earth also upon which I stood, and the beast of the field and the fowls of heaven and the fish of the waters, and also man walking forth upon the face of the earth in majesty and in the strength of beauty[,] whose power and intelligence in governing the things which are so exceeding great and marvelous, even in the likeness of Him who created them. And when I considered upon these things[,] my heart exclaimed, "Well hath the wise man said it is a fool that saith in his heart there is no God." My heart exclaimed [that] all these bear testimony and bespeak an omnipotent and omnipresent power, a being who maketh laws and decreeth and bindeth all things in their bounds who filleth eternity, who was and is and will be from all eternity to eternity. And when I considered all these things and that that being seeketh such to worship Him as worship Him in spirit and

Red= 1842/1843, Joseph Smith   Purple = 1843, Levi Richards

Aqua = 1843, David White   Lavender = 1844, Alexander Neibaur   Gray = Added for ease of reading in truth, therefore I cried unto the Lord for mercy[,] for there was none else to whom I could go and to obtain mercy.

JS—H 11 While I was laboring in this state of perplexity under the extreme difficulties caused by the contests of these parties of religionists, I was one day reading the Epistle of James, first chapter and fifth verse, which reads: *If any of you lack wisdom, let him ask of God, that giveth to all men liberally, and upbraideth not; and it shall be given him.*

JS—H 12 This was cheering information to [me]: tidings that gave [me] great joy to guide [me] to the path in which [I] should walk. It was like a light shining forth in a dark place. [Moreover,] never did any passage of scripture make a deeper impression [or] come with more power to the heart of man than this did at this time to mine. It seemed to enter with great force into every feeling of my heart. I reflected on it again and again, knowing that if any person needed wisdom from God, I did; for how to act I did not know, and unless I obtained[4] more wisdom than I then had, I would never know which were right; for the teachers of religion of the different sects interpreted [and] understood the same passages of scripture so differently as to destroy all confidence in settling the question by an appeal to the Bible. [I] now saw that if [I] inquired of God, there was not only a possibility, but a probability; yea, more, a certainty, that [I] should obtain a knowledge, which of all the doctrines was the

JOSEPH SMITH JR.

doctrine of Christ, and which of all the churches was the church of Christ.

JS—H 13 At length I came to the conclusion that I must either remain in darkness and confusion, or else I must do as James directs, that is, ask of God. I at length came to the determination to "ask of God," concluding that if He gave wisdom to them that lacked wisdom, and would give liberally, and not upbraid, [He] would not refuse to verify His promise to me[, and] I might venture. [I] considered this passage an authorization for [me] to solemnly call upon [my] creator[,] to present [my] desires before Him with the sure hope of certain success. I knew not who was right or who was wrong[,] and I considered it of the first importance that I should be right in matters that involve eternal consequences. Information was what I most desired at this time, and with a fixed determination to obtain it, I called on the Lord for the first time.

JS—H 14 So, in accordance with this, my determination to ask of God, being thus perplexed in mind, I retired to the woods to make the attempt and bowed down before the Lord. It was on the morning of a beautiful, clear day, early in the spring of eighteen hundred and twenty. It was the first time in my life that I had made such an effort,[5] for amidst all my anxieties I had never as yet made the attempt to pray vocally.

JS—H 15 I immediately went out into the woods where my father had a clearing and went to the stump where I had stuck my

Blue = 1832, Joseph Smith | Green = 1835, Joseph Smith | Black = 1838, Joseph Smith
Brown = 1840, Orson Pratt | Orange = 1841, Joseph Smith | Teal = 1842, Orson Hyde

axe when I had quit work. After I had retired to the place where I had previously designed to go, having looked around me, and finding myself alone, in the place above stated or, in other words, I made a fruitless attempt to pray. I kneeled down and began to offer up the desires of my heart to God. I had scarcely done so, when immediately I was seized upon by some power which entirely overcame me, and had such an astonishing influence over me as to bind my tongue so that I could not speak. My tongue seemed to be swollen in my mouth, so that I could not utter. I heard a noise behind me like some one walking towards me. Thick darkness gathered around me, and it seemed to me for a time as if I were doomed to sudden destruction. The adversary made several strenuous attempts to cool the passion of [my] soul. He clouded [my] mind with doubts and brought to [my] mind all sorts of improper images to prevent [me] from attaining the object of [my] endeavors; I strove again to pray, but could not; the noise of walking seemed to draw nearer, [and] I sprang upon my feet and looked round, but saw no person or thing that was calculated to produce the noise of walking.

JS—H 16 But, exerting all my powers [and] every energy to call upon God to deliver me out of the power of this enemy which had seized upon me, and at the very moment when I was ready to sink into despair and abandon myself to destruction—not to an imaginary ruin, but to the power [and] influence of some actual being from the unseen world, who had such marvelous power as I had never before felt in any being—just at this moment of great alarm, I kneeled again, my mouth was opened and my tongue loosed [and as] I called on the Lord in mighty prayer, the dark cloud soon parted and light and peace filled [my] frightened heart [or in other words,] the overflowing mercy of our God came to uplift [me] and impart new impetus to [my] failing strength. I saw a pillar of light [or] fire exactly over my head, which exceeded the brightness of the dazzling sun in his meridian splendor, [and it] came down from above, which at first seemed to be at a considerable distance. As it drew nearer, it increased in brightness and magnitude, so that by the time that it reached the tops of the trees, the whole wilderness, for some distance around, was illuminated in a most glorious and brilliant manner. [I] expected to have seen the leaves and boughs of the trees consumed, as soon as the light came in contact with them; but, perceiving that it did not produce that effect [I] was encouraged with the hopes of being able to endure its presence, which descended gradually until it fell upon me. It presently rested down upon me and filled me with unspeakable joy. [Indeed] it continued descending, slowly, until it rested upon the earth, and [I] was enveloped in the midst of it.

JS—H 17 It no sooner appeared than I found myself delivered from the enemy which held me bound. When the light rested upon me it produced a peculiar sensation throughout [my]

Blue = 1832, Joseph Smith Green = 1835, Joseph Smith Black = 1838, Joseph Smith
Brown = 1840, Orson Pratt Orange = 1841, Joseph Smith Teal = 1842, Orson Hyde

whole system; and, immediately [my] mind was caught away, from the natural objects with which [I] was surrounded; and [I] was enwrapped in a heavenly vision. [Furthermore,] I was filled with the Spirit of God, [and the] Lord opened the heavens upon me.[6] A personage appeared in the midst of this pillar of flame, which was spread all around and yet nothing consumed, [having a] light complexion, blue eyes, a piece of white cloth drawn over his shoulders, his right arm b[are]. After a while another personage soon appeared to the side of the first [who was] like unto the first. I saw two[7] heavenly [and] angelic Personages who exactly resembled each other in features, and likeness, [and] whose brightness and glory defy all description, standing above me in the air. One of them spake unto me, calling me by name and said to the second, pointing to the other—*This is My Beloved Son. Hear Him!* He testified also unto me that Jesus Christ is the Son of God. They informed [me] that [my] prayers had been answered and that the Lord had decided to grant [me] a special blessing. And He spake unto me saying, ["]Joseph[,] my son, thy sins are forgiven thee, go thy way[,] walk in my statutes and keep my commandments, behold I am the Lord of glory. I was crucified for the world that all those who believe on my name may have eternal life.["][8]

JS—H 18 My object in going to inquire of the Lord was to ascertain[9] which of all the sects was right, that I might know which to join. Consequently[,] as soon as possible [and] no sooner,

Blue = 1832, Joseph Smith Green = 1835, Joseph Smith Black = 1838, Joseph Smith
Brown = 1840, Orson Pratt Orange = 1841, Joseph Smith Teal = 1842, Orson Hyde

therefore, did I get possession of myself, so as to be able to speak, than I addressed this second person[10] who stood above me in the light, saying, ["]O Lord, what Church shall I join[?" And asking] which of all the sects was right (for at this time it had never entered into my heart that all were wrong [because] I supposed that one of them [to be right]).[11]

JS—H 19 I was answered that I must join none of them, for they were all wrong; and the Personage who addressed me said that all their creeds were an abomination in his sight; that those professors were all corrupt because all of them were mistaken in their doctrine and not recognized by God as his church and kingdom [because] the Everlasting Covenant was broken; that: "The world lieth in sin at this time and none doeth good, no[,] not one. They have turned aside from the Gospel and keep not my commandments. They draw near to me with their lips, but their hearts are far from me, they teach for doctrines the commandments of men, having a form of godliness, but they deny the power thereof[,] and mine anger is kindling against the inhabitants of the earth to visit them according to this ungodliness and to bring to pass that which hath been spoken by the mouth of the prophets and Apostles. Behold and lo, I come quickly[,] as it [is] written of me, in the cloud clothed in the glory of my Father."

JS—H 20 He again forbade me to join with any of them. [I] was further commanded to wait patiently until a future time,

receiving a promise that the true doctrine of Christ and the fullness of the gospel should be revealed to [me]; and many other things did He say unto me, which I cannot write at this time. I saw many angels in this vision. When I came to myself again, I found myself lying on my back, looking up into heaven. Peace and calm filled [my] mind. When the light had departed, I had no strength; I endeavored to arise but felt uncommonly feeble[,] but soon recovering in some degree, I went home. And as I leaned up to the fireplace, mother inquired what the matter was. I replied, "Never mind, all is well—I am well enough off." I then said to my mother, "I have learned for myself that Presbyterianism is not true." My soul was filled with love, and for many days I could rejoice with great joy; the Lord was with me, but [I] could find none that would believe the heavenly vision; nevertheless[,] I pondered these things in my heart, but after many days I fell into transgression and sinned in many things[,] which brought wound[s] upon my soul, and there were many things which transpired that cannot be written. It seems as though the adversary was aware, at a very early period of my life, that I was destined to prove a disturber and an annoyer of his kingdom; else why should the powers of darkness combine against me? Why the opposition and persecution that arose against me, almost in my infancy? I was about 14 years old when I received this first communication.

Red= 1842/1843, Joseph Smith Purple = 1843, Levi Richards
Aqua = 1843, David White Lavender = 1844, Alexander Neibaur Gray = Added for ease of reading

CONCLUSION

The lessons the First Vision can teach are many. Joseph saw his visionary experience with new eyes as the years passed and shared it differently, often depending on his audience. We similarly digest and interpret the First Vision differently at various times in our spiritual growth. As such, several observations can be made after reading the harmony.

1. The harmonized account vividly portrays the struggle and near desperation Joseph experienced as he sought to discern the truth and learn which church he should join. We can also see how Joseph's search for a true church relates to his quest for personal righteousness and forgiveness of sin. Seeing the accounts as a unified narrative gives a new appreciation for his sincerity of heart and the length of time he yearned for that special knowledge. Joseph's "humble

JOSEPH SMITH FIRST VISION STAINED GLASS

prayer"[1] was not a hasty supplication but one he spent a great deal of time preparing to offer.

2. The harmony provides a vivid portrayal of a fourteen-year-old boy's frightening encounter with Satan. There is a heightened sense of the bitter anguish and terror Joseph felt as the enemy of all righteousness attempted to thwart that which Joseph Smith himself later said he was foreordained to accomplish.[2] Reading this difficult component of the experience all at once provides a startling reminder of the reality of evil and of our need to be rescued from our fallen condition.

3. The highlight of the harmony is the appearance of the Father and the Son. We are presented with a deeper sense of awe and reverence of this spectacular moment. We are also reminded that Joseph saw the first two members of the Godhead, as well as many other angels—how many we do not know. It is not hard to imagine a scene somewhat similar to the angels that heralded the birth of the Son of God (Luke 2:13–14).[3]

4. Much has been written about the differences in Joseph's accounts of the appearance of heavenly beings. Some have drawn the conclusion that there is an attempt on his part to deceive. With the accounts conflated into one, however, a case is made for the unity that exists among the accounts relative to the appearance of the Deity. As the experience in the Sacred Grove is painted in vivid colors, we are able to visualize successive appearances in the theophany.

5. For the first time in one place, all the recorded words spoken by the Lord Jesus Christ to Joseph are combined. The divine message given to reassure the Prophet can also comfort us. We begin to glimpse the comprehensive answer Joseph received, as well as gain an appreciation for the events of the Restoration that followed the First Vision. The Lord's teachings to Joseph provide important context to the Lord's well-known instruction that Joseph was not to join any of the churches of his day. Further, we see the reason those religious leaders only had "a form of godliness, but they den[ied] the power thereof": the everlasting covenant was broken (JS—H 1:19). The Lord instructed Joseph about the everlasting covenant and informed him that he would be the means of restoring the fulness of the gospel to the earth. The harmonization showcases enough information to see that there was much related to Joseph's future call and prophetic assignment given to him that day that we still do not have.

6. When we read the harmony, we begin to consider reasons and motivations for sharing different elements at one time or another in new ways. For instance, in the earliest years of the Church, the beginning or foundational experience most commonly shared among members and with investigators was the coming forth of the Book of Mormon, not the First Vision. Thus, in his 1832 account, Joseph doesn't spend time underscoring his search for a true church to join but instead emphasizes a very personal component of the First Vision:

his own quest for forgiveness of his sins. However, the 1838 account is introduced as being written to set the record straight and respond to falsehoods that were being spread "by evil-disposed and designing persons" (JS—H 1:1). Because the 1838 account was to be published to the world, it seems logical that the Prophet Joseph would not focus so much on his personal need for redemption as he did in the 1832 account, but rather emphasize on the message that affects the entire human race—the fact that he was to "join none of [the churches], for they were all wrong" (JS—H 1:19).

As mentioned previously, when Joseph Smith shared the First Vision with others, he emphasized details suited to the occasion and purpose.[4] Just as a musician might employ different instruments, or a painter different brushes, Joseph had different reasons for sharing his experience, and as the audience changed, so did his emphasis. On some occasions, the Prophet shared his experience when asked by visitors, such as in 1835. In other instances, he shared because he was fulfilling a commandment that "there shall be a record kept" by completing his history and the history of the Church (D&C 21:1). We know that Joseph Smith shared his First Vision on other occasions, but we do not have records of those instances. Based on the historical evidence and Joseph's practice, there is every reason to believe he shared elements that are different from what we currently have to suit the particular situation in which he was sharing.

A common criticism against Joseph Smith, as alluded to earlier, is that the various accounts of the First Vision are so different that he must have manufactured the experience. However, James Allen wrote that "the differences in the accounts may be grossly overemphasized, for the truth is that there is wide and credible agreement in detail among them all."[5] It is remarkable how well the accounts, though told to different people for varying circumstances, work together to create a harmony of truth. The accounts, in fact, seem to sustain and reinforce one another.

For some, there will be more to gain from this harmony than to simply read the different accounts in one narrative. This harmony will allow readers to recognize nuances that might have previously escaped their attention. It will be a different experience for each reader. Together, these accounts create a vivid image of the various known elements that took place "on the morning of a beautiful, clear day, early in the spring" of 1820 (JS—H 1:14). Read all at once, the harmony paints a scene of what the experience might have felt like, looked like, and sounded like for the fourteen-year-old boy called to be a prophet. Indeed, in our mind's eye, we almost feel as if we are looking over Joseph's shoulder as he has this transcendent and sacred experience.

INVITATION AND WITNESS

In February 1832, Joseph Smith and Sidney Rigdon received section 76 of the Doctrine and Covenants, also known as "the Vision," at the John Johnson farm in Hiram, Ohio. In this revelation, an empowering doctrine is revealed with an accompanying invitation. At the conclusion of sharing what was seen, Joseph reveals that others may prepare to have the same wondrous experience. Invitingly, the vision is "only to be seen and understood by the power of the Holy Spirit, which God bestows on those who love Him, and purify themselves before Him; to whom He grants this privilege of seeing and knowing for themselves; that through the power and manifestation of the Spirit, while in the flesh, they may be able to bear His presence in the world of glory" (D&C 76:116–18). Several years later, the Prophet renewed the invitation by teaching that "God hath not revealed anything to Joseph, but what He will make known unto the Twelve and even the least Saint may know all things as fast as he is able to bear them."[6] Joseph was not possessive of what God had revealed to him. Indeed, Joseph beckons his listeners to share in his experiences. Though we will not be called upon to open a dispensation like Joseph, we are invited to become personal and powerful witnesses of his experience.

Thus, this harmonization and the subsequent invitation allow us a greater understanding of Joseph's mission and his first of many visions and visitations. We are encouraged not to only observe the young Prophet in the grove, but to kneel beside him and learn for ourselves if what he said he saw and heard actually happened. As the late Joseph Fielding McConkie wrote, "Our doctrine is not simply that if we live righteously we can receive revelation; rather it is that if we live right there is no power that can prevent our receiving it . . . all who would claim to the promise of salvation must do so as prophets or prophetesses. Each must claim a personal dispensation of the gospel. All who profess a testimony of the gospel must have a knowledge of saving truths that stands independent of the revelations given to others."[7] The vision is Joseph's, but as believers in his divine calling, we are invited into it. Indeed, the harmonization is an additional illustration that as followers of the Prophet, we have no excuse to remain outside the grove. Our view should be and can be unique—beside Joseph Smith in the Sacred Grove.

The experience of the First Vision is not just Joseph Smith's story. It is a universal story. In it are elements common to all truth seekers. The First Vision vividly illustrates the steps all must go through to learn spiritual truths. We must yearn for the truth and be willing to submit ourselves to God's answer no matter what. God is willing to give us light if we are worthy and prepared to receive it. The Lord, through Joseph's experience, teaches us that we must search and pray for answers. We learn there is sometimes bitter opposition before receiving those answers. And learn that light does not come all at once but descends gradually. Our invitation and obligation is to accept that light and to then prepare ourselves to receive additional light and truth—"until the perfect day" (D&C 50:24).

Joseph Smith is the prototype for our dispensation. He demonstrates to all that our Heavenly Father will honor the promise made during the Meridian of Time: "If any of you lack wisdom, let him ask of God, that giveth to all men liberally, and upbraideth not; and it shall be given him" (James 1:5). It is for us to seek and ask, to knock and receive. Joseph is the perfect witness that God does answer our prayers. It is now for each of us to find our own Sacred Grove and personally ask of God.

An early intention in this endeavor to compile the harmonization was to assemble the various known contemporary accounts of the First Vision in such a way that it would be akin to what one might hear from Joseph himself. The reality is that such an undertaking is not possible unless it were done by the Prophet himself. It would be wonderful if Joseph Smith were with us today and could nod approvingly at the arrangement of the phrases in this harmony. After reading the harmonization, however, there is a self-evident realization: Joseph would not sit and watch someone make a feeble attempt to cobble the accounts into a single composition. He might point us to the official account of the First Vision as it has been canonized, approved by the Lord, and accepted by the membership of the Church.[8]

There is another possibility that is equally intriguing: the Prophet Joseph Smith might simply tell us about his experience in his own words. He would likely share new details and give different emphasis to some elements over others. Following the pattern he established during his ministry, and in addition to the any details he might share, the Prophet's principle message would be just as powerful and relevant as it has always been:

- He saw the Father and the Son.
- The called him by name and answered his prayer.
- He went on and obeyed God's command and heard His Only Begotten Son.

Through His inspired and authorized mouthpiece, we are invited to receive blessings as we follow the same command: "Hear Him!" Then, as it has before, light would gradually descend and fill the grove of trees, and also our minds and hearts.

INTRODUCTION ENDNOTES

1 Joseph used this phrase in his journal entry on 14 November 1835. Dean C. Jessee, Mark Ashurst-McGee, and Richard L. Jensen, eds., *Journals, Volume 1: 1832–1839,* Vol. 1 of the Journals series of *The Joseph Smith Papers,* edited by Dean C. Jessee, Ronald K. Esplin, and Richard Lyman Bushman (Salt Lake City: Church Historian's Press, 2008), 100.

2 The author is heavily indebted to Milton V. Backman Jr. It was his book, *Joseph Smith's First Vision,* now out of print, that originally exposed the author to the different accounts of the First Vision. While reading Backman's book and many First Vision accounts in the Sacred Grove in June 2003, the author first wondered if there was a harmonized version of the accounts available to read. The challenge to actually create the harmony came as part of an assignment from W. Jeffrey Marsh when the author took his Teachings of Joseph Smith class in the fall of 2003 at Brigham Young University. This book was subsequently entered as a paper into the BYU Religious Education Student Symposium and was presented in February 2004. There are many scholars who have written about the First Vision accounts, which made the present work possible. For instance, the writings of James B. Allen, Milton V. Backman Jr., Richard L. Bushman, Steven C. Harper, Dean Jessee, Joseph Fielding McConkie, Robert L. Millet, Craig J. Ostler, Eldon Watson, and John W. Welch have made significant contributions to current understandings of the First Vision in general and the various accounts specifically. The author of this work is heavily indebted to them and others.

3 Richard L. Bushman, *Joseph Smith: Rough Stone Rolling* (New York: Alfred E. Knopf, 2005), 40.

4 To read the accounts in their entirety, see the author's website or consult the references in the endnotes. Another source is Steven C. Harper's *Joseph Smith's First Vision: A Guide to the Historical Accounts* (Harper does not include the Coray version in his book though he does include another 1835 account which is not in this compilation; see footnote 11). Backman's *Joseph Smith's First Vision* included many of the accounts in an appendix and is an important book for First Vision studies.

5 For information about the similarities and differences in many of the following accounts, readers are recommended to James Allen's articles in the autumn 1966 volume of *Dialogue* and the April 1970 of *The Era*. These and other articles on the First Vision have recently been republished in *Exploring the First Vision*, edited by Steven C. Harper and Samuel Alonzo Dodge. Because the articles in *Exploring the First Vision* will be more accessible for interested readers, all references will be to Harper and Dodge's book as appropriate. These articles are invaluable to understanding the significance of the accounts.

6 Karen Lynn Davidson, David J. Whittaker, Richard L. Jensen, and Mark Ashurst-McGee, eds. *Histories, Volume 1: Joseph Smith Histories, 1832–1844*. Vol. 1 of the Histories series of *The Joseph Smith Papers,* edited by Dean C. Jessee, Ronald K. Esplin, and Richard Lyman Bushman (Salt Lake City: Church Historian's Press, 2012), 11–13. Milton V. Backman, Jr., *Joseph Smith's First Vision: Confirming Evidences and Contemporary Accounts*, 2nd ed. rev. (Salt Lake City: Bookcraft, 1980), 155–57.

7 Though the 1832 account is the first time the Prophet formally records the events of the First Vision, it is likely that an early revelation made reference to it. "After it was truly manifested unto this first elder [Joseph Smith] that *he had received a remission of his sins*, he was entangled again in the vanities of the world." (D&C 20:5; emphasis added.)

8 Joseph Smith, *The Personal Writings of Joseph Smith*, 2nd edition, ed. Dean C. Jessee (Salt Lake City: Deseret Book, 2002), 10.

9 *JSP*, H1:10.

10 *JSP,* H1:6, cf. 10–13; Jessee, *Writings* 2002, xx, 10–12, 15.

11 *JSP,* J1:87–95; Backman, 158–59. For a repurposed version of this account for Joseph's history see JSP, H1:115–16.

A few days after Robert Matthews' visit Joseph again recounted his experience in the sacred grove on November 14 to a man named Erastus Holmes. The entry states that Joseph shared "a brief relation of my experience while in my juvenile years, say from 6 years old up to the time I received the first visitation of Angels which was when I was about 14 years old . . ." (JSP, J1:100.) Though an important evidence that Joseph shared his experience with others, the journal entry does not contain additional details to warrant inclusion in the harmony.

12 *JSP,* J1:95. For information on Robert Matthews see JSP, J1:86–87.
13 *JSP*, J1:87; Jessee, *Writings* 2002, 104, 108; Backman, 158.
14 *JSP*, J1:55–56; Joseph Smith, *The Personal Writings of Joseph Smith*, compiled and edited by Dean C. Jessee (Salt Lake City: Deseret Book, 1984), 651 fn. 27; James B. Allen, "Eight Contemporary Accounts of Joseph Smith's First Vision—What Do We Learn From Them?," *Era*, April 1970, 5.
15 *JSP,* H1:204–20; Backman, 160–65.
16 This account was canonized with the rest of the Pearl of Great Price in a General Conference of The Church of Jesus Christ of Latter-day Saints on 10 October 1880. See *Journal History*, 10 October 1880, Church Historian's Office, Salt Lake City. Journal History of the Church, 10 October 1889, 4, LDS Church Archives (chronology of typed entries and newspaper clippings, 1830–present), also available on Selected Collections from the Archives of The Church of Jesus Christ of Latter-day Saints, 2 vols. Provo, Utah: Brigham Young University Press, 2002, vol. 2, DVD 8, microfilm copy in Harold B. Lee Library, Brigham Young University, Provo, Utah.
17 Steven C. Harper, *Joseph Smith's First Vision: A Guide to the Historical Accounts* (Salt Lake City: Deseret Book, 2012), 44.
18 Allen in Dodge and Harper's *Exploring the First Vision*, 294–95.
19 Allen and Welch in Dodge and Harper's *Exploring the First Vision*, 54.
20 *JSP*, H1:520–24; Backman, 170–72.
21 *JSP*, H1:517.
22 Allen in Dodge and Harper's *Exploring the First Vision*, 290–94. Allen demonstrates that though the evidence is not conclusive the First Vision was likely shared with converts as early as 1831. Certainly with Pratt's 1840 publication the First Vision is becoming a teaching point in Church proselyting.
23 Though Pratt's name was read along with eleven others he was serving a mission at the time and therefore not present for the 14 February ordinations. After he arrived in Kirtland he was ordained on 26 April 1835.
24 *Times and Seasons*, Vol. 2, No. 19, 2 August 1841, 502.
25 Allen and Welch in Dodge and Harper's *Exploring the First Vision*, 59.
26 *JSP*, H1:517, fn. 3.
27 *JSP*, H1:209–15.

28 This account was discovered in the Church Archives in 2005 as a part of the extensive cataloguing done by the capable scholars of the Joseph Smith Papers project. See *JSP*, H1:200.

29 Joseph Smith, *The Words of Joseph Smith: The Contemporary Accounts of the Nauvoo Discourses of the Prophet Joseph*, compiled and edited by Andrew F. Ehat and Lyndon W. Cook. Provo: BYU Religious Studies Center, 1980, 419, fn. 2.

30 *JSP*, H1:201.

31 *JSP*, H1:200. The statement is dated 1869.

32 http://josephsmithpapers.org/paperSummary/orson-hyde-ein-ruf-aus-der-wste-1842-extract (accessed May 20, 2014); Backman, 173–75.

33 *JSP*, H1:492–94.

34 *JSP*, H1:489; Backman, 168–69.

35 Though this history, including the account of the First Vision, was never used in Barstow's history of New Hampshire, it was published, however, in the *Times and Seasons, vol. 3*, No. 9, March 1, 1842, 706–10, the official LDS newspaper of the time.

36 *JSP*, H1:492.

37 http://josephsmithpapers.org/paperSummary/levi-richards-journal-11-june-1843-extract (accessed May 20, 2014).

38 Joseph Smith, *The Words of Joseph Smith: The Contemporary Accounts of the Nauvoo Discourses of the Prophet Joseph*, compiled and edited by Andrew F. Ehat and Lyndon W. Cook. Provo: BYU Religious Studies Center, 1980, 215.

39 http://josephsmithpapers.org/paperSummary/interview-21-august-1843-extract (accessed May 20, 2014); Backman, 176.

40 Joseph Smith, *The Papers of Joseph Smith*, Vol. 1, compiled and edited by Dean C. Jessee (Salt Lake City: Deseret Book, 1989), 438

41 *Opening the Heavens: Accounts of Divine Manifestations*, 1820–1844, 49.

42 http://josephsmithpapers.org/paperSummary/alexander-neibaur-journal-24-may-1844-extract (accessed May 20, 2014); Backman, 177.

43 Jessee, *Papers*, 459; Hugh Nibley, "Censoring Joseph Smith's Story," *Improvement Era* (July, 1961), 522. Of interest, Nibley says in his article that he is the great-grandson of Neibaur, and that he found the entry one day almost by accident while reading his great-grandfather's journal.

44 *Times and Seasons*, Vol. 2, No. 19, 2 August 1841, 502, has an article announcing his arrival from Europe and his services.

45 Jessee, *Papers*, 459.

46 Joseph Smith to William W. Phelps, 27 November 1832, Church History Library, The Church of Jesus Christ of Latter-day Saints, Salt Lake City, Utah. Available online at josephsmithpapers.org. Spelling and punctuation modernized. I am grateful to Steven Harper for introducing me to this letter in his book *Joseph Smith's First Vision*.

47 Letter from George A. Smith to Wilford Woodruff, 21 April 1856, published in *The Words of Joseph Smith*, xvi.

48 James B. Allen, *Exploring the First Vision*, 300; "The Significance of Joseph Smith's First Vision in Mormon Thought," *Dialogue: A Journal of Mormon Thought*, Vol. 1, No. 3 (Autumn 1966), 42.

THE FIRST VISION ENDNOTES

1 According to the 1832 account, Joseph was 12 years old when "my mind became seriously impressed with regard to the all important concerns for the welfare of my immortal soul." For a fuller discussion of when Joseph Smith began to search for truth, see Allen and Welch in Dodge and Harper's *Exploring the First Vision*, 41–89; and Harper, *Joseph's Smith First Vision*, 23–30.

2 The 1838 account has "so."

3 According to the 1832 account, Joseph was in the 16th year of his age, when he was in the "attitude of calling upon the Lord." Of course, in the 1838 account (JS—H) Joseph says he was in his 15th year, which would put him at the age of 14. For a more thorough discussion on the Prophet's age, see Allen and Welch in Dodge and Harper's *Exploring the First Vision*, 63–65.

4 The 1838 account has "could get."

5 The 1838 account has "attempt."

6 In the 1832 account also states, "I saw the Lord." See JSP J1:12–13, and fn. 45 on 13.

7 Joseph, in the various accounts he gave, did not always tell his audience precisely who came in response to his prayer. In the 1832 account, he only makes reference to "the Lord," and says he was "filled with the spirit of God." In his 1835 telling of the First Vision, Joseph says one "personage appeared" and "another personage soon

appeared like unto the first." The 1838 telling of the story tells us that there were two personages that seemingly appeared at the same time. In the 1842 Wentworth account, Joseph wrote he "saw two glorious personages." See also Allen in Dodge and Harper's *Exploring the First Vision*, 297.

A fascinating tertiary account is found in an 1893 journal entry of Charles Walker, a pioneer. While in a Church meeting, Walker reports that he heard John Alger say that "when he, John was a small boy he heard the Prophet Joseph relate his vision of seeing The Father and the Son, That God touched [Joseph's] eyes with his finger and said, 'Joseph this is my beloved Son hear him.' As soon as the Lord had touched his eyes with his finger he immediately saw the Savior. After the meeting, a few of us questioned him about the matter and he told us at the bottom of the meeting house steps that he was in the House of Father Smith in Kirtland when Joseph made this declaration, and that Joseph while speaking of it put his finger to his right eye, suiting the action with the words so as to illustrate and at the same time impress the occurrence on the minds of those unto whom he was speaking. We enjoyed the conversation very much, as it was something that we had never seen in church history or heard of before." (A. Karl Larsen and Katherine Miles Larsen, eds., *Diary of Charles Lowell Walker*, Vol. 2 [Logan: Utah State University Press, 1980], 755–56.)

8 Based on the different accounts of the First Vision, it is presumed that Jesus Christ, the Son, is speaking to Joseph Smith and declaring his sins to be forgiven. This conclusion is also dependent on scriptural patterns that it is the Son who declares forgiveness. At the unveiling of a bronze statue by artist Avard T. Fairbanks in the Joseph Smith Building on the campus of Brigham Young University entitled "The Vision" on October 17, 1997, Elder Henry B. Eyring taught that it was Jesus Christ who announced that Joseph's sins were forgiven. See "The Vision" at http://yfacts.byu.edu/Article?id=112 (accessed May 14, 2014).

9 The 1838 account has "know."

10 The 1838 account has "asked the Personages."

11 The conclusion of this sentence in the 1838 account—"and which I should join"—was removed to avoid repetition.

CONCLUSION ENDNOTES

1 "Joseph Smith's First Prayer," George Manwaring, *Hymns of the Church of Jesus Christ of Latter-day Saints*, 26.
2 *History of the Church* 6:364.
3 For other scriptural precedents of a host of angels—often a choir—praising the Godhead at their appearance, see 1 Nephi 1:8, Job 38:7; Revelation 5:11; and Mormon 7:7. King Benjamin told his people he desired to join the heavenly choir at some point when he died (Mosiah 2:28).
4 As Allen wrote, "The several variations in these and other accounts would seem to suggest that, in relating his story to various individuals at various times, Joseph Smith emphasized different aspects of it and his listeners were each impressed with different things. This, of course, is to be expected, for the same thing happens in the re-telling of any story." Allen in Dodge and Harper's *Exploring the First Vision*, 300.
5 Allen and Welch in Dodge and Harper's *Exploring the First Vision*, 46.
6 *The Words of Joseph Smith*, Joseph Smith, *The Words of Joseph Smith: The Contemporary Accounts of the Nauvoo Discourses of the Prophet Joseph*, compiled and edited by Andrew F. Ehat and Lyndon W. Cook. Provo: BYU Religious Studies Center, 1980, 4.
7 Joseph Fielding McConkie, *Prophets and Prophecy* (Salt Lake City: Bookcraft, 1988), 90–91.
8 The 1838 account appears to have been what Joseph Smith wanted as the official record of the First Vision.

ABOUT THE AUTHOR

Matthew B. Christensen was raised in Edmonds, Washington, with his three siblings by his loving parents, Bryan and Carol Christensen. Now residing in Provo, Utah, he is married to Talia Soria Christensen and they have four beautiful children. Matthew attended BYU and received his Bachelor's degree in public relations and his Master's degree in public management. Matthew is a donor liaison at LDS Philanthropies, a department of the Presiding Bishop's Office in the LDS Church. He is passionate about the restored gospel and enjoys reading, learning, and discussing the revelations of the Restoration. He has served in a variety of callings and embraces all teaching opportunities he gets. Some of his other experiences include teaching Book of Mormon and Doctrine & Covenants courses at BYU as an adjunct instructor. Though this is Matthew's first publication, he is no stranger to the process. He contributed to researching and writing the last eleven books of the late Joseph Fielding McConkie.

0 26575 15044 5